Nihil Obstat, Arthur J. Scanlan, S.T.D., Censor Liborum
Imprimatur ✠ Francis Cardinal Spellman,
Archbishop of New York
Cum Permissu Superiorum

William J. Hirten Co., Cumberland, RI

GLORIA
Children's Books

# THE TEN COMMANDMENTS OF GOD

## God's Laws for Us

by Daniel A. Lord, S.J.

# These are God's Ten Commandments that He gave to Moses:

First God said, "I am the Lord, Your God, who brought you out of the land of Egypt, out of the house of bondage."
Then He gave us His Commandments.

God knew that if His children
obeyed these Commandments,
they would all be happy.
He knew that if they disobeyed,
they would all be sad.
Let us see what these
Commandments mean.

## *I. I am the Lord your God... you shall have no other gods before me.*

God made us to know,
love and serve Him
and to be happy with Him
forever in Heaven.
Jesus, You are my one Lord and God,
and I love You.

## *II. You shall not take the name of the Lord your God in vain.*

We must honor God's Holy Name
and only speak His Name with
reverence and praise.
Jesus, Jesus, Jesus – I honor
Your Holy Name.

## *III. Remember to keep holy the Sabbath Day.*

From the beginning, God has taught
us to rest one day a week.
As Catholics, Sunday is a special day
of rest and prayer with our families,
especially by going to Mass.
Lord, help me to worship You
by always going to Mass on Sunday
and making it a special day of
prayer and rest.

# *IV. Honor your father and mother.*

We must love, respect,
and obey our parents.
When we obey our parents,
we obey God and please Him.
Jesus, teach me to love and obey my
parents as You were obedient to Your
parents, Mary and Joseph.
Help my parents to
guide me in Your ways.

## *V. You shall not kill.*

Our lives belong to God, and we
must take care of ourselves.
We must also be a good example to
others and treat them
as we want to be treated.
Thank you God for my life and help
me to love everyone as
You love me.

## *VI. You shall not commit adultery.*

We will be happy if we learn the virtues of purity and modesty. Blessed Virgin Mary and St. Joseph, help me to be pure in all I see, hear, say and do.

## *VII. You shall not steal.*

We must be fair and honest,
we should also share what
belongs to us with others.
Jesus, I trust in You
to take care of me and to
provide for my needs.

## *VIII. You shall not bear false witness against your neighbor.*

We must never harm another
by saying false or unkind
things about them.
We must always tell the truth.
Lord, help me not to judge so that
I will not be judged,
help me to always tell the truth
even if I may be punished.

## *IX. You shall not covet your neighbor's wife.*

In this commandment,
God is telling us to never willingly think impure things. Only when a man and a woman are married can they make a family as God intends. Lord, please help all husbands and wives to love each other and help everyone to honor the Sacrament of Marriage. Help me to be pure and to dress appropriately.

# *X. You shall not covet your neighbor's goods.*

We should desire the things of God,
like grace and virtue.
We should not wish for things that do
not belong to us.
We must be willing to
share our things.
Jesus, help me not to be
selfish with my things
or envious of what others have.

# *How To Be Good*

To be good, you must obey the Commandments of God. Keep your mind and heart pure and holy. Shun bad movies, bad video games, bad books, bad companions and you will be God's Child on earth and enjoy your future life in Heaven with Him forever.

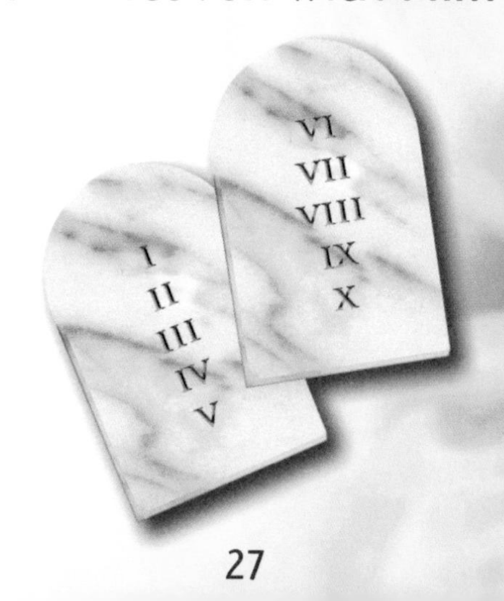